Diaper Duty

Korena Glover

Order this book online at www.trafford.com
or email orders@trafford.com

Most Trafford titles are also available at major online book retailers.

Printed in Victoria, BC, Canada.

ISBN: 978-1-4269-2872-7 (sc)

Library of Congress Control Number: 2010903751

Our mission is to efficiently provide the world's finest, most comprehensive book publishing service, enabling every author to experience success. To find out how to publish your book, your way, and have it available worldwide, visit us online at www.trafford.com

Trafford rev. 4/28/2010

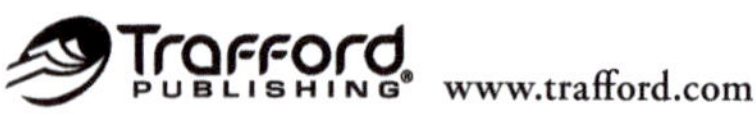

www.trafford.com

North America & international
toll-free: 1 888 232 4444 (USA & Canada)
phone: 250 383 6864 • fax: 812 355 4082

My Mommy & Daddy

MOMMY'S FULL NAME IS ______________________________

SHE IS FROM ______________________________

SHE WORKS FOR ______________________________

MY DADDY'S FULL NAME IS ______________________________

HE IS FROM ______________________________

HE WORKS FOR ______________________________

MOMMY AND DADDY MET

____

____

____

WE LIVE IN ______________________________

BECAUSE OF ____________________'S JOB IN THE U.S. ____________________

MY ____________________CHOSE THE MILITARY BECAUSE,

____

____

All About Mommy

All About Daddy

WOMB CAMP

MY FIRST PICTURE

MOMMY FIRST VISITED DR. ______________________ AT ____________ HOURS ON THIS

DATE___________________AND FOUND OUT SHE WAS PREGNANT.

MY ETA WAS EXPECTED TO BE ____

DADDY & MOMMY CELEBRATED BY____

____

____

THE FIRST PEOPLE MOMMY & DADDY SHARED THE GOOD NEWS WITH WERE:

____

____

____

____

MOMMYS BODY CHANGED A LOT WHILE I WAS AT WOMB CAMP, SHE ATE SOME SILLY FOODS LIKE

____

PICTURE OF MOMMY'S BELLY

MOMMY FIRST FELT ME MOVE ON ____________________________

SONOGRAM PICTURE

AT AROUND 20 WEEKS MOMMY & DADDY FOUND OUT I WAS A ____________________

SOME OF THE NAMES THEY LIKED:

____

____

____

AS ANY GOOD SOLDIER OR SAILOR KNOWS, GEAR IS AN IMPORTANT PART OF READINESS.

MOMMY HAD A SPECIAL "RED TEAM" WHO THREW US A WONDERFUL BABY SHOWER. MEMBERS OF THIS SPECIAL TEAM WERE

____

____

____

____

BABY SHOWER PICS

FRIENDS AND FAMILY FROM ALL OVER GATHERED TO CELEBRATE.

GUESTS	RELATIONSHIP	GIFTS

SOME OF OUR FAVORITE GIFTS: ______________________

BABY SHOWER GAMES WE PLAYED WERE ______________________

LABOR DAY

I ARRIVED ON____________________AT________________HOURS

I WAS BORN AT ________________HOSPITAL IN ____________________

MY FULL NAME IS ____________________________________

MY WEIGHT WAS ______LB______OZ. AND I WAS ________IN LONG.

MOMMY WAS IN LABOR FOR ____________HOURS.

PICTURES OF MY ARRIVAL, NEWSPAPER ANNOUNCEMENT

Tiny Fingers & Tiny Toes

FOOTPRINT & HANDPRINT PAGE

Letter From Mommy

Letter From Daddy

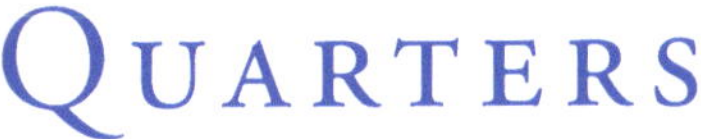

QUARTERS

HOME LIFE CHANGED A LOT WHEN WE LEFT THE HOSPITAL. I ARRIVED HOME ON

____

THIS IS MY NEW ROOM. MOMMY AND DADDY DECORATED IT WITH LOVE.

I ATE EVERY ____________ HOURS, SO MOMMY & DADDY DIDN'T GET MUCH SLEEP.

I HAD VISITORS FROM ALL OVER.

PICTURES OF FRIENDS & FAMILY WITH BABY

My First Spring

MY FIRST SPRING I WAS ________________ MONTHS OLD.

I MET THE EASTER BUNNY FOR THE FIRST TIME.

SOME OF MY FAVORITE THINGS TO DO AT THIS AGE WERE:

PICTURES

MY BIGGEST ACCOMPLISHMENTS THIS SPRING WERE:

MY FIRST SUMMER

MY FIRST SUMMER I WAS__________________ MONTHS OLD.

WE SPENT MOST OF THE SUMMER

____

____

I CELEBRATED MY FIRST INDEPENDENCE AND LABOR DAY.

____

SOME OF MY FAVORITE THINGS TO DO AND SEE AT THIS AGE WERE:

____

____

PICTURES OF MY SUMMER FUN

MY BIGGEST ACCOMPLISHMENTS OF THE SUMMER WERE:

____

____

My First Fall

MY FIRST FALL I WAS ____________________ MONTHS OLD.

I HAD MY FIRST HALLOWEEN & THANKSGIVING.

SOME OF MY FAVORITE THINGS TO DO AND SEE AT THIS AGE WERE:

____

____

PICTURES OF FAMILY/HOLIDAY FUN

MY BIGGEST ACCOMPLISHMENTS OF THE FALL WERE:

____

____

____

My First Winter

MY FIRST WINTER I WAS ________________ MONTHS OLD.

I CELEBRATED MY FIRST CHRISTMAS AND NEW YEAR.

SOME OF MY FAVORITE THINGS TO DO AT THIS AGE WERE:

PICTURES

MY BIGGEST ACCOMPLISHMENTS THIS WINTER WERE:

Family Tree

Baby Firsts

I FIRST SMILED AT ______________(MONTHS)

MY FIRST COO WAS AT _______________(MONTHS)

MY FIRST LAUGH WAS AT ___________(MONTHS)

MY FIRST WORD WAS ________________________ AT ____________________________ (MONTHS).

I COULDN'T WAIT TO GET MOVING, I TOOK ON CRAWLING AT ________________________ (MONTHS).

I TOOK MY FIRST STEPS AT __________________________ (MONTHS).

MY FIRST FOODS WERE ____

I LOVED _______________________ BUT NOT ____________________________SO MUCH.

MY FIRST ADVENTURE WAS

____

____

____

MY FAVORITE TOYS ARE ____

____

MY FAVORITE TIME OF DAY IS ____

BECAUSE ____

SOME OTHER FAVORITE FIRSTS FOR MOMMY & DADDY ARE:

____

____

____

____

My Precious Moments

DATE:

DATE:

DATE:

DATE:

DATE:

My Precious Moments

DATE:

DATE:

DATE:

DATE:

DATE:

My Precious Moments

DATE:

DATE:

DATE:

DATE:

DATE:

My Precious Moments

DATE:

DATE:

DATE:

DATE:

DATE:

Watch Me Grow

BIRTH TO I YR DR VISITS HEIGHT/WEIGHT

Now & Then

THE YEAR I WAS BORN:

THE PRICE OF A GALLON OF MILK WAS ____________

THE PRICE OF A GALLON OF GAS WAS ______________

THE PRICE OF A LOAF OF BREAD WAS _____________

THE AVERAGE PRICE OF A CAR WAS _______________

A HOUSE COST AROUND ___________________

DIAPERS COST _____________________

POP CULTURE

YOU WERE COOL IF YOU HAD ____ THE YEAR I WAS BORN

POPULAR ACTORS WERE____

BIG MOVIES WERE____

THE NEWEST AND BEST GADGETS WERE ____

____

OTHER COOL TRENDS WERE:

____

____

____

POLITICS

THE YEAR I WAS BORN ______________________________ WAS PRESIDENT.

______________________________ WAS VICE PRESIDENT.

HEADLINES IN THE NEWS WERE: ______________________________

____

THE ECONOMY WAS: ______________________________

NEWS PAPER ARTICLE, PICTURE, SPACE FOR KEEPSAKE

My First Birthday

I TURNED ONE ON ______________________ THE __________ DAY OF ________________________

THE WEATHER WAS ____.

WE HAD MY FIRST PARTY AT ____.

THE THEME WAS____.

PICTURE OF ME

FRIENDS AND FAMILY WHO ATTENDED WERE:

____

____

____

____

____

____

I GOT SOME WONDERFUL GIFTS LIKE: ____

____

____

____

Duty Stations

TO REMEMBER PLACES I'VE LIVED AND FRIENDS I'VE MADE.

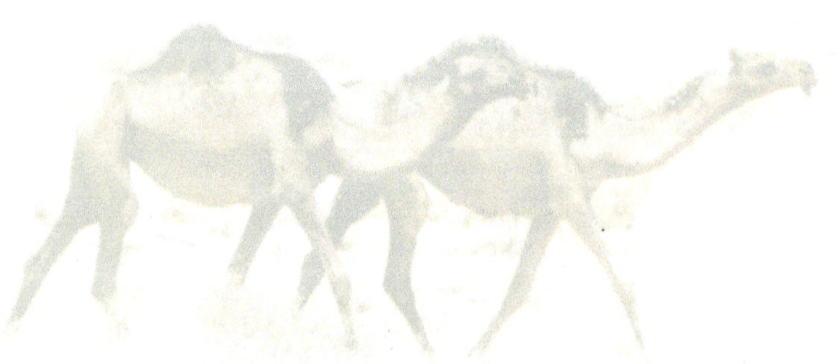

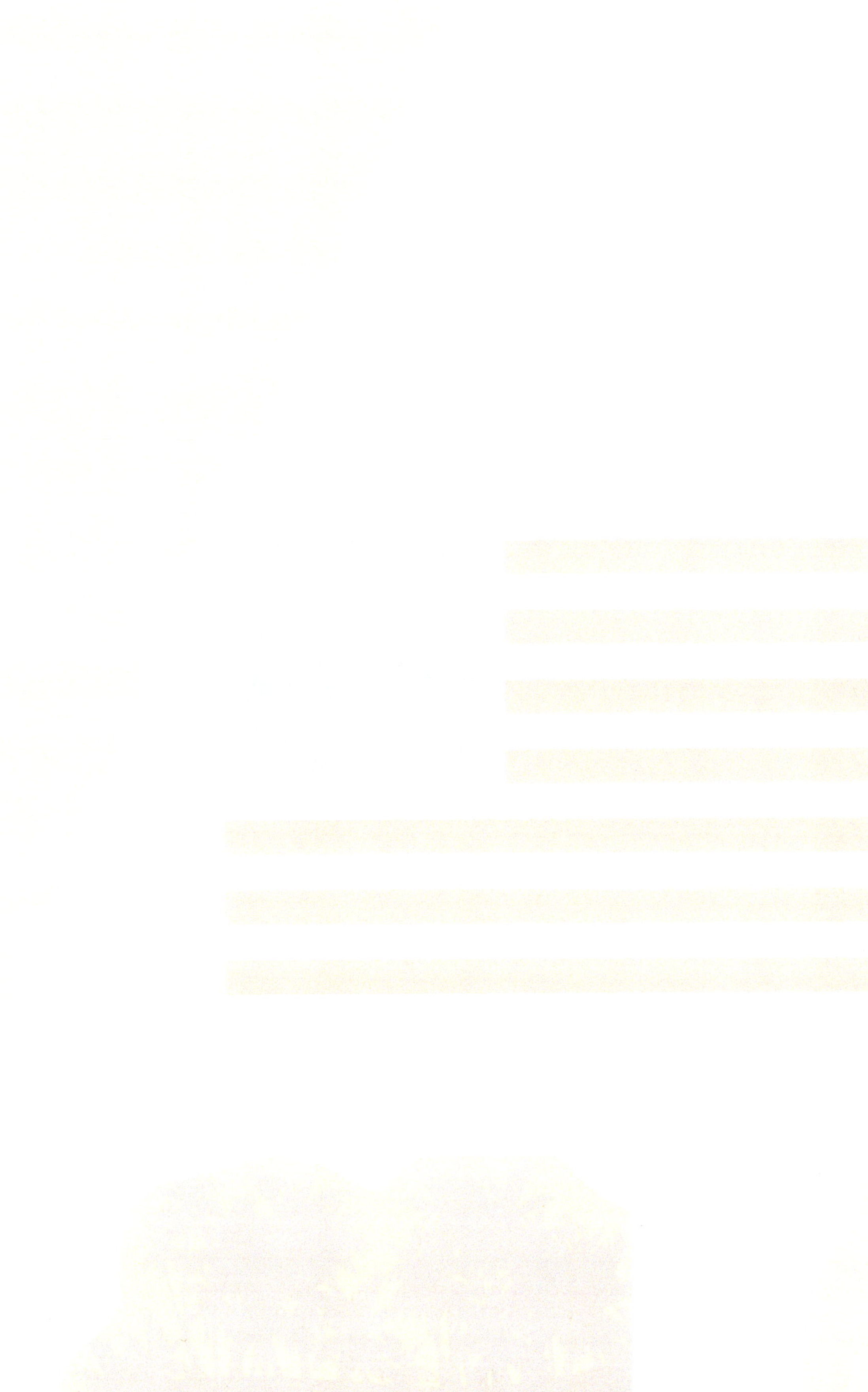

Interesting Travels

"SCRAPBOOK" MATERIALS OR PICTURES OF VACATIONS/MILITARY TRAVELS

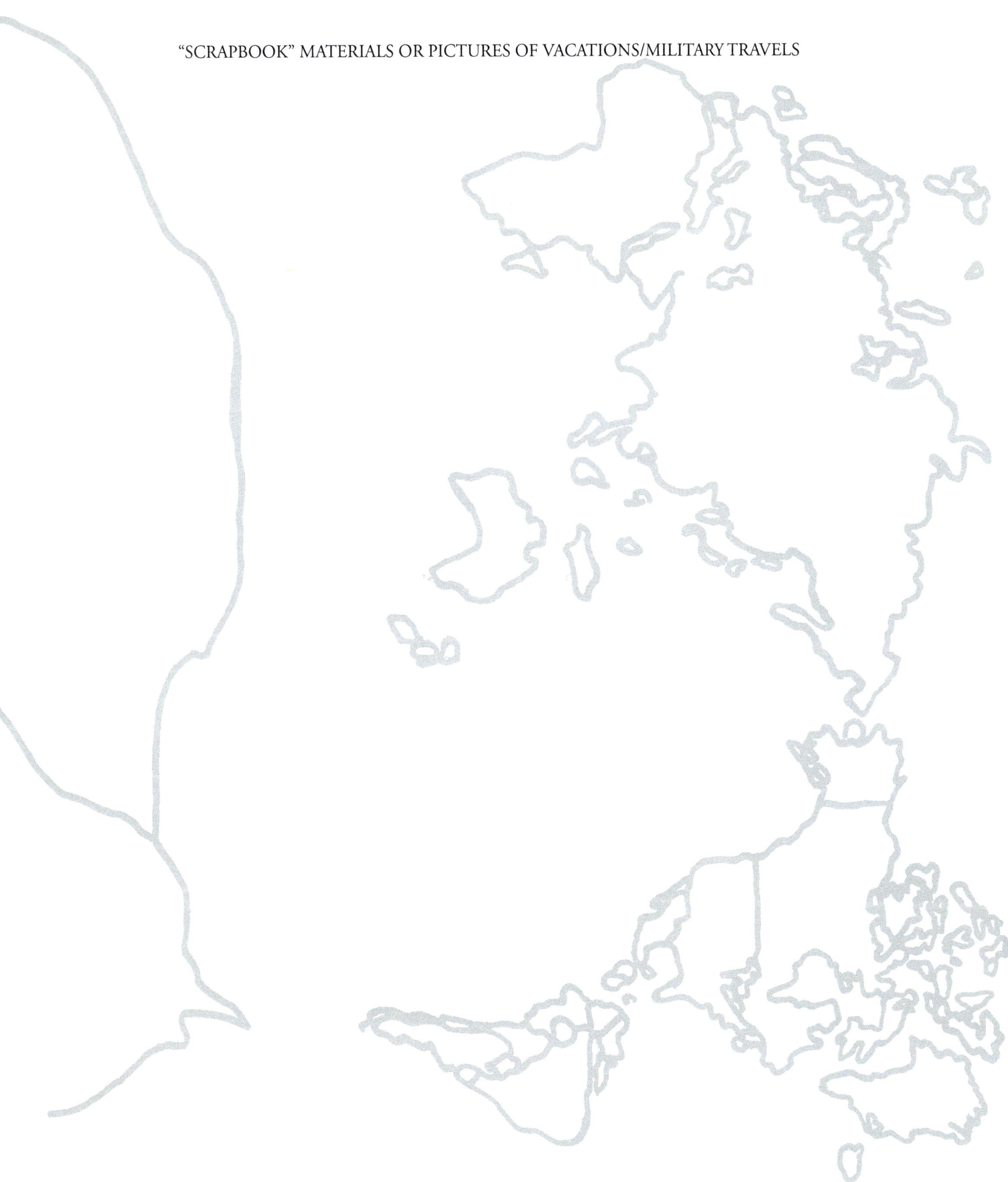

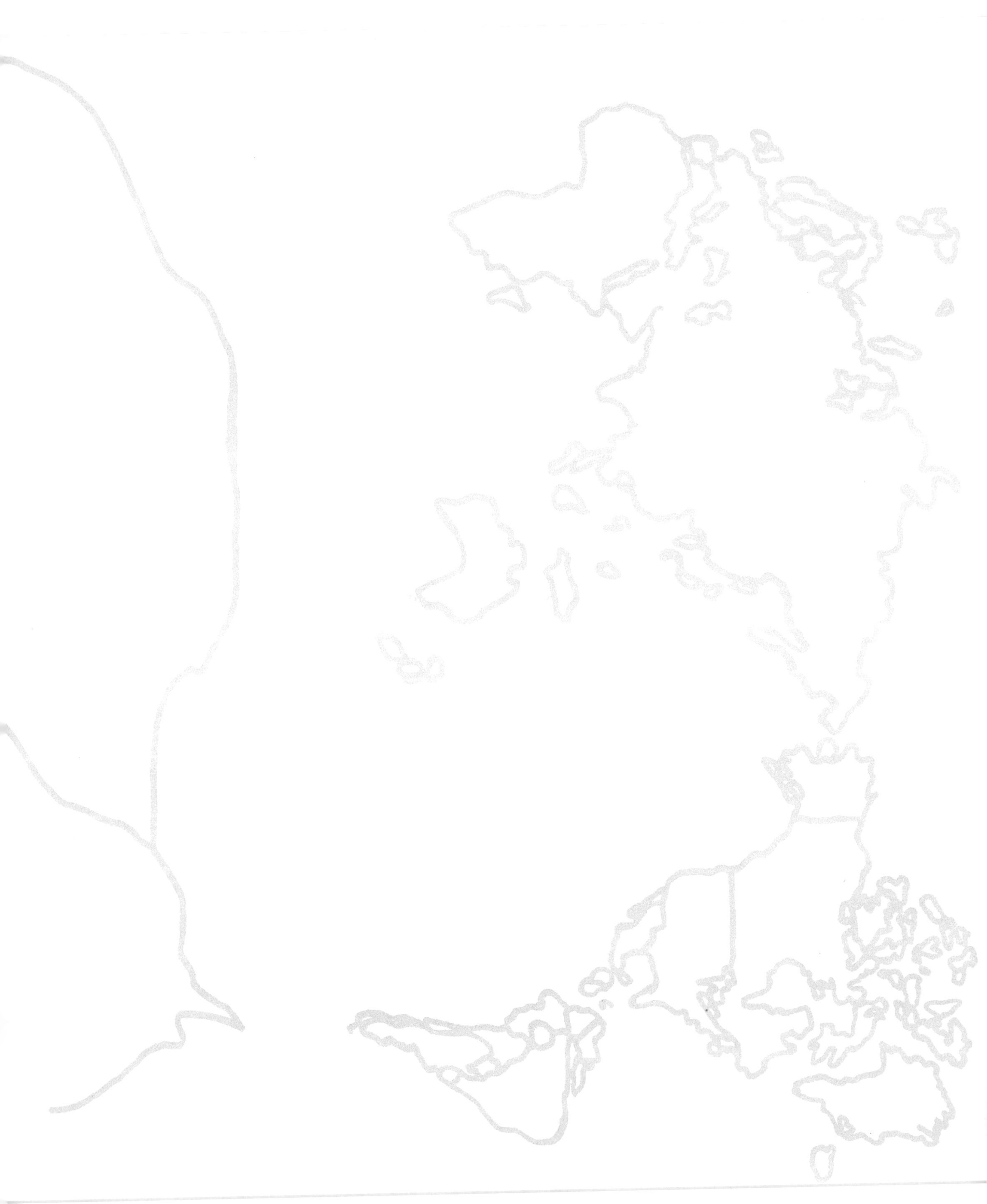

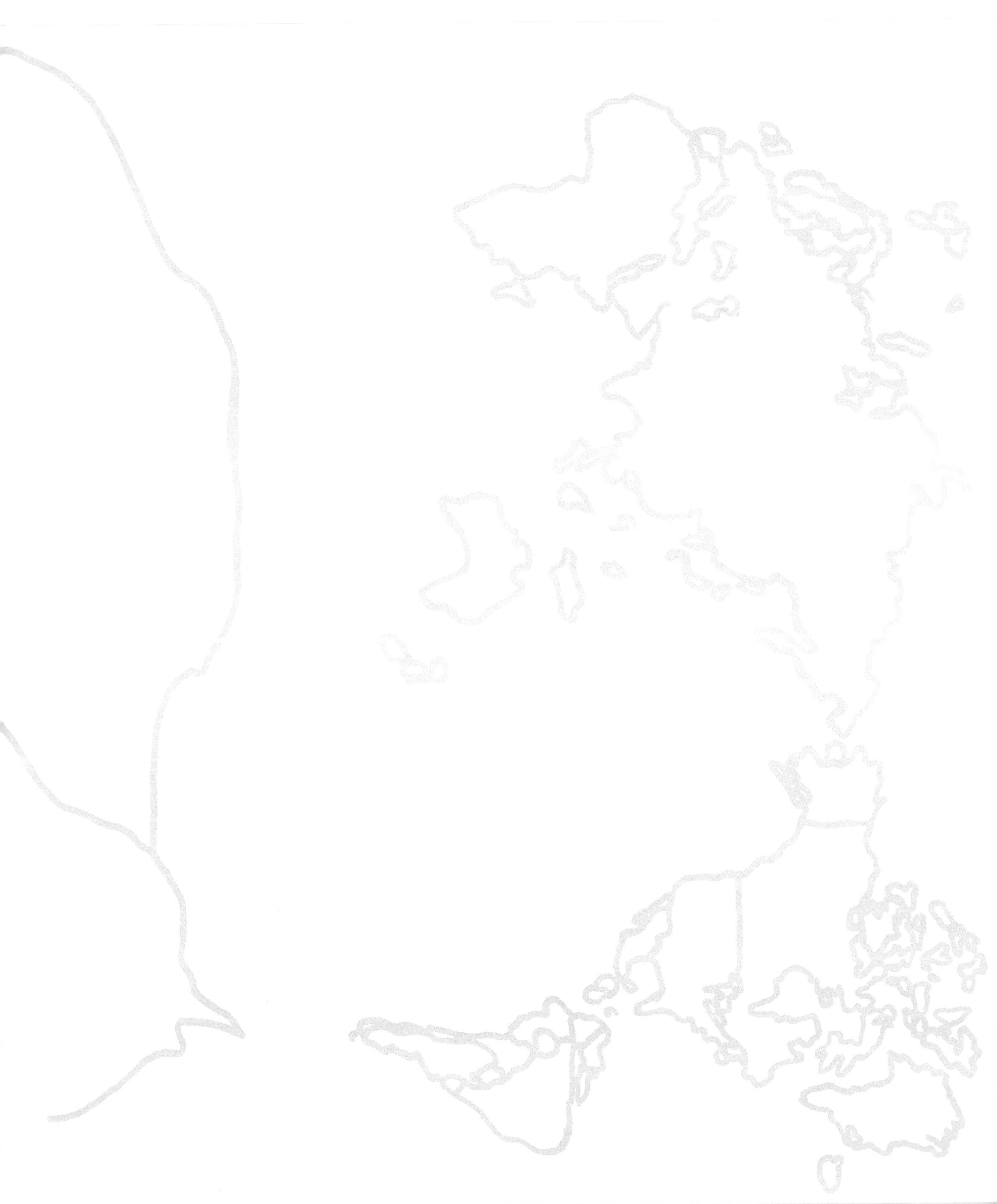

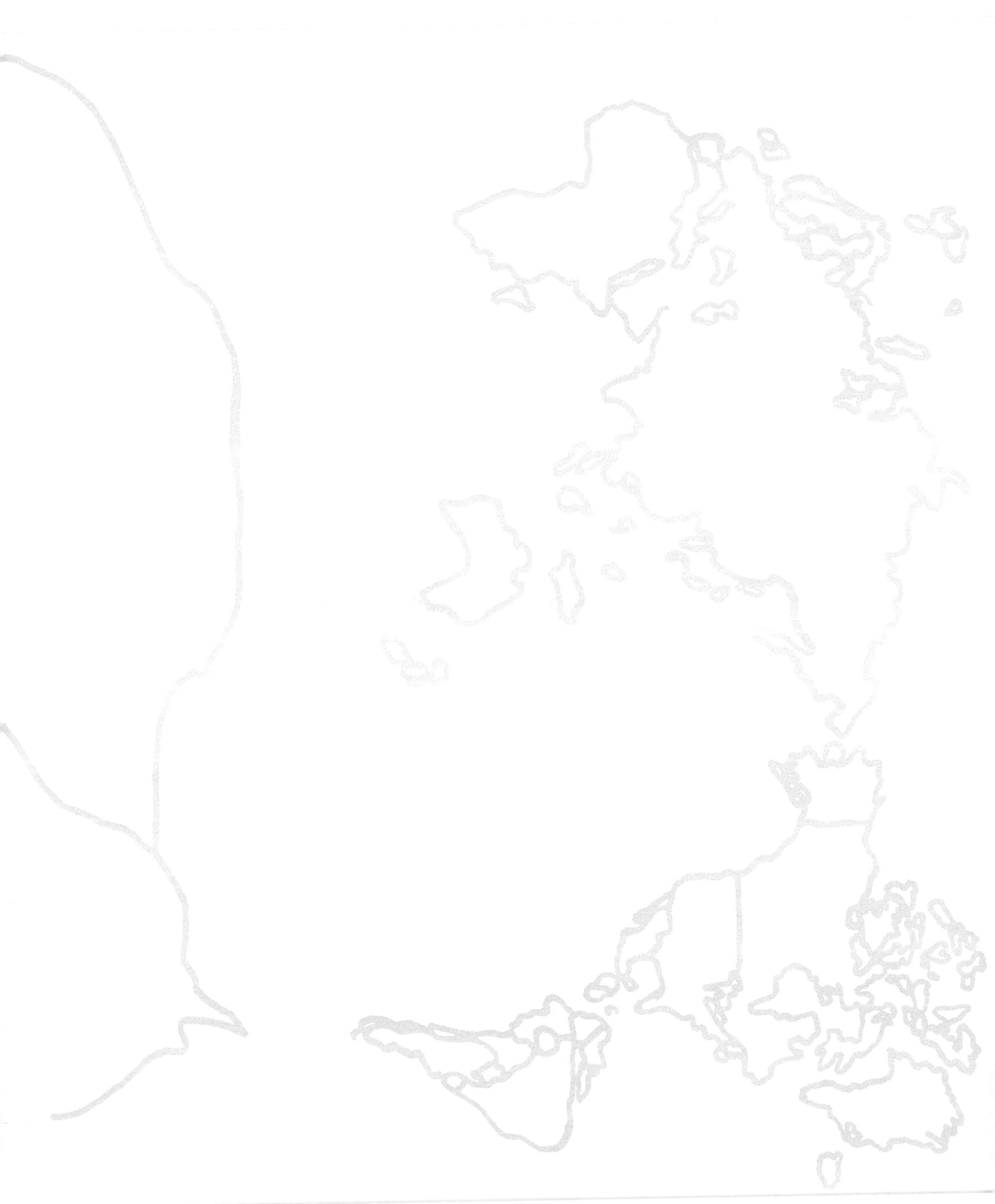

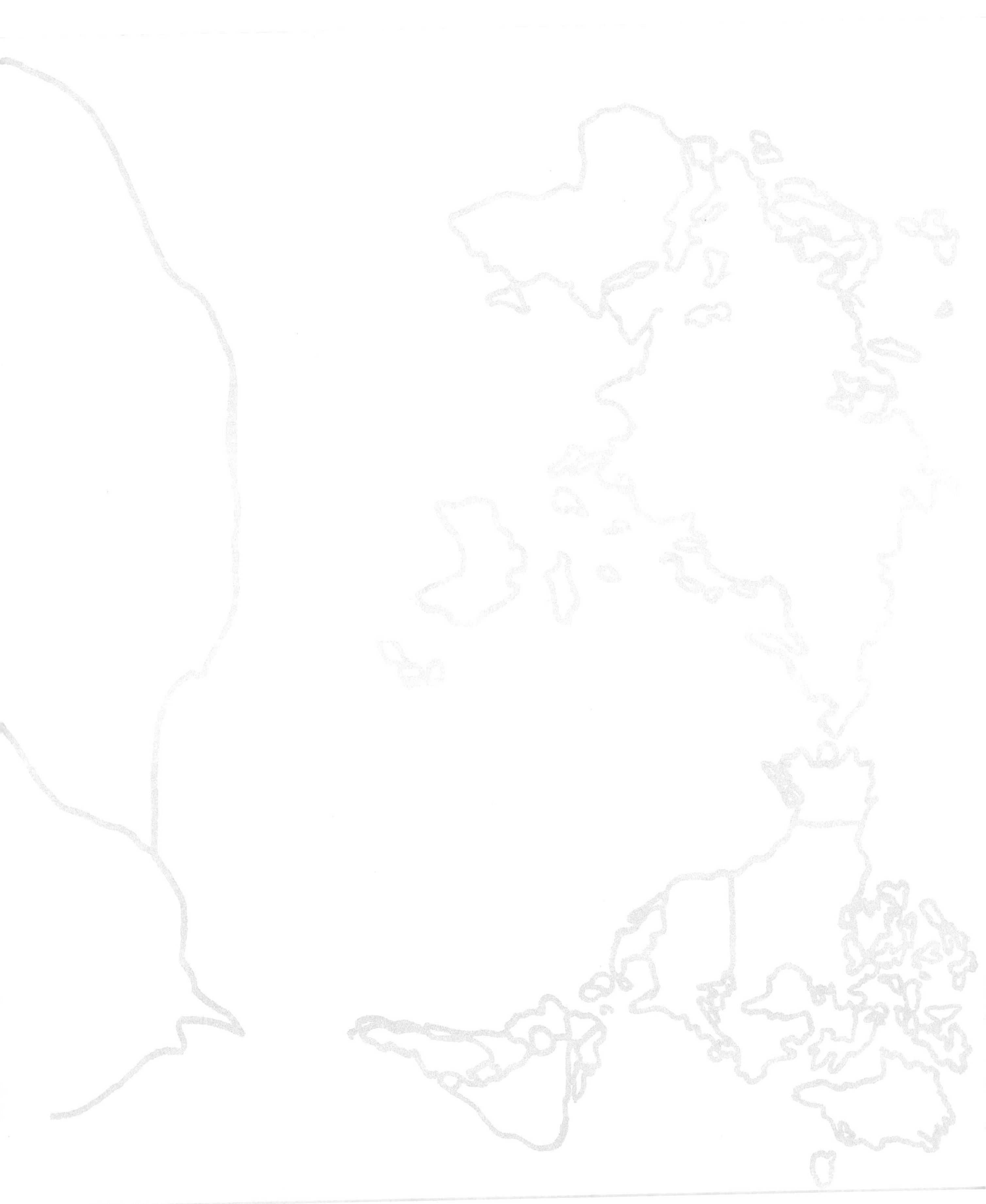

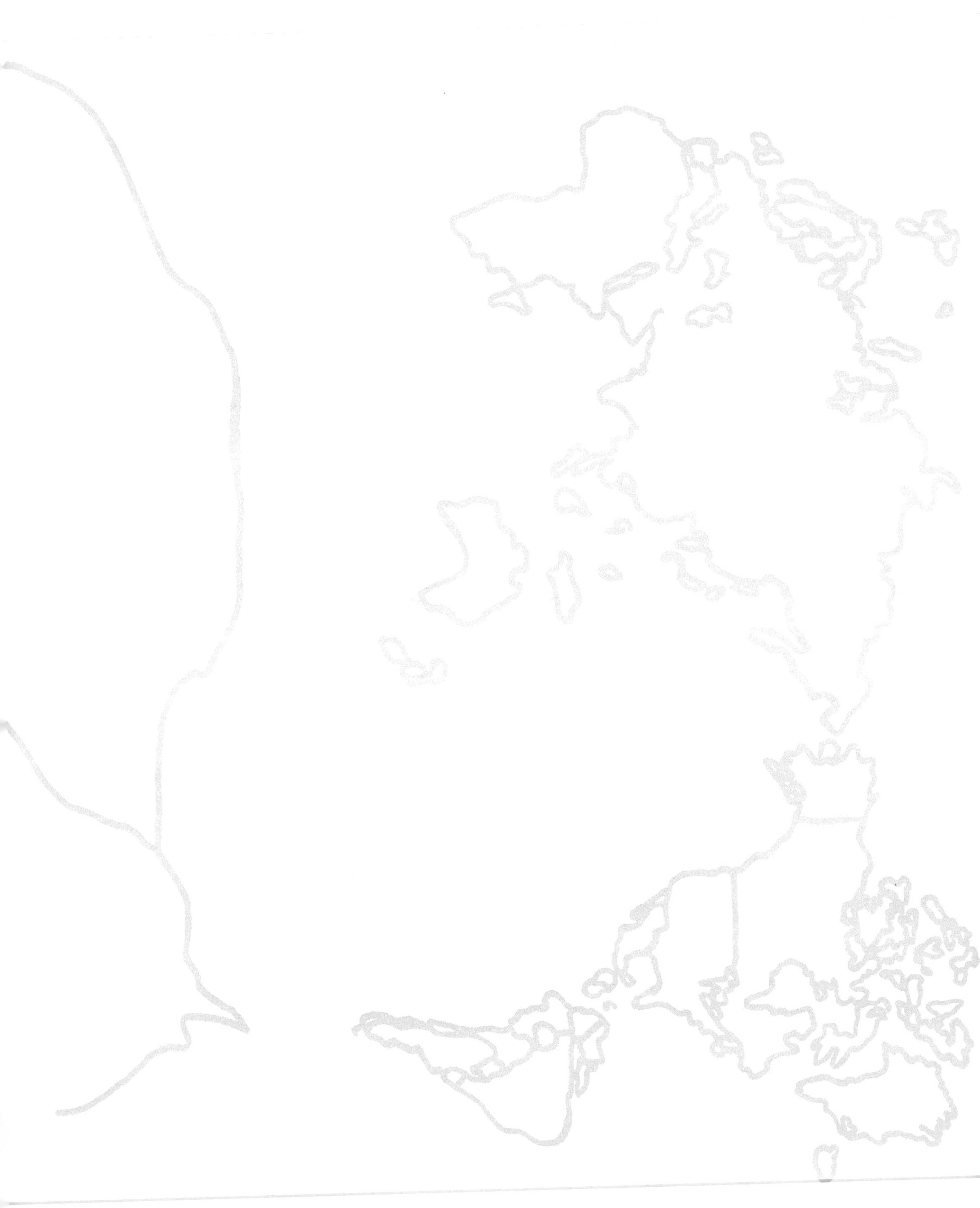

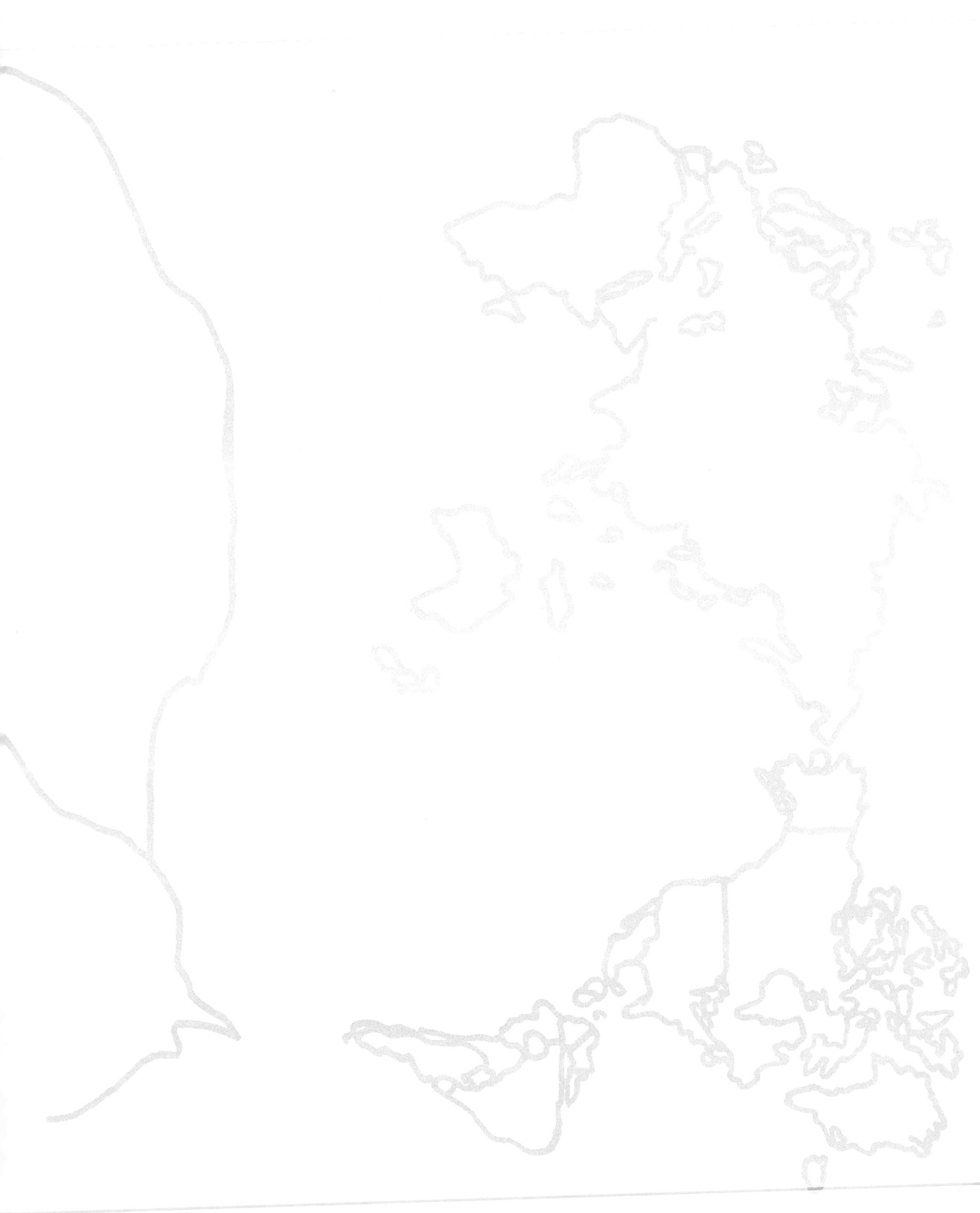

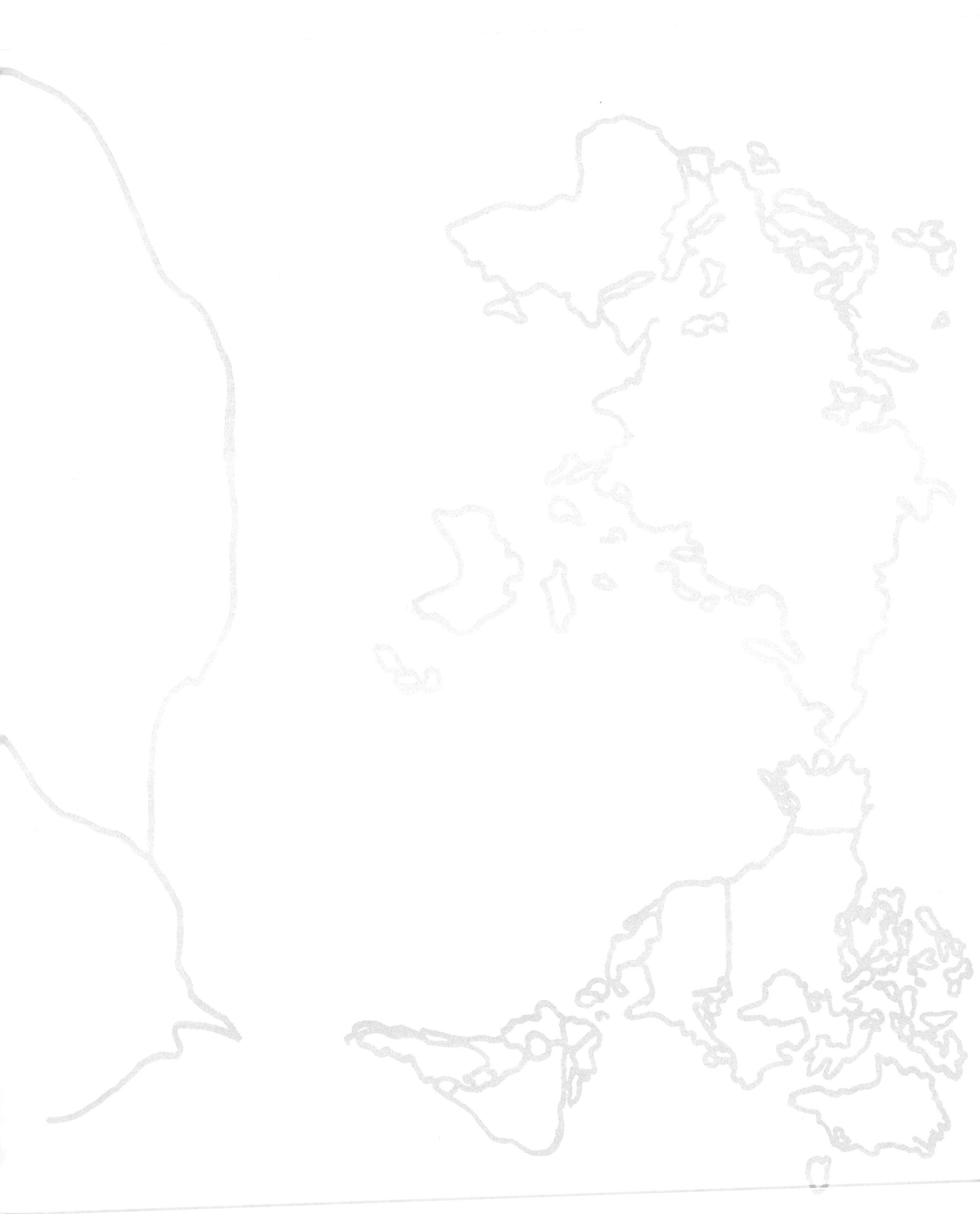

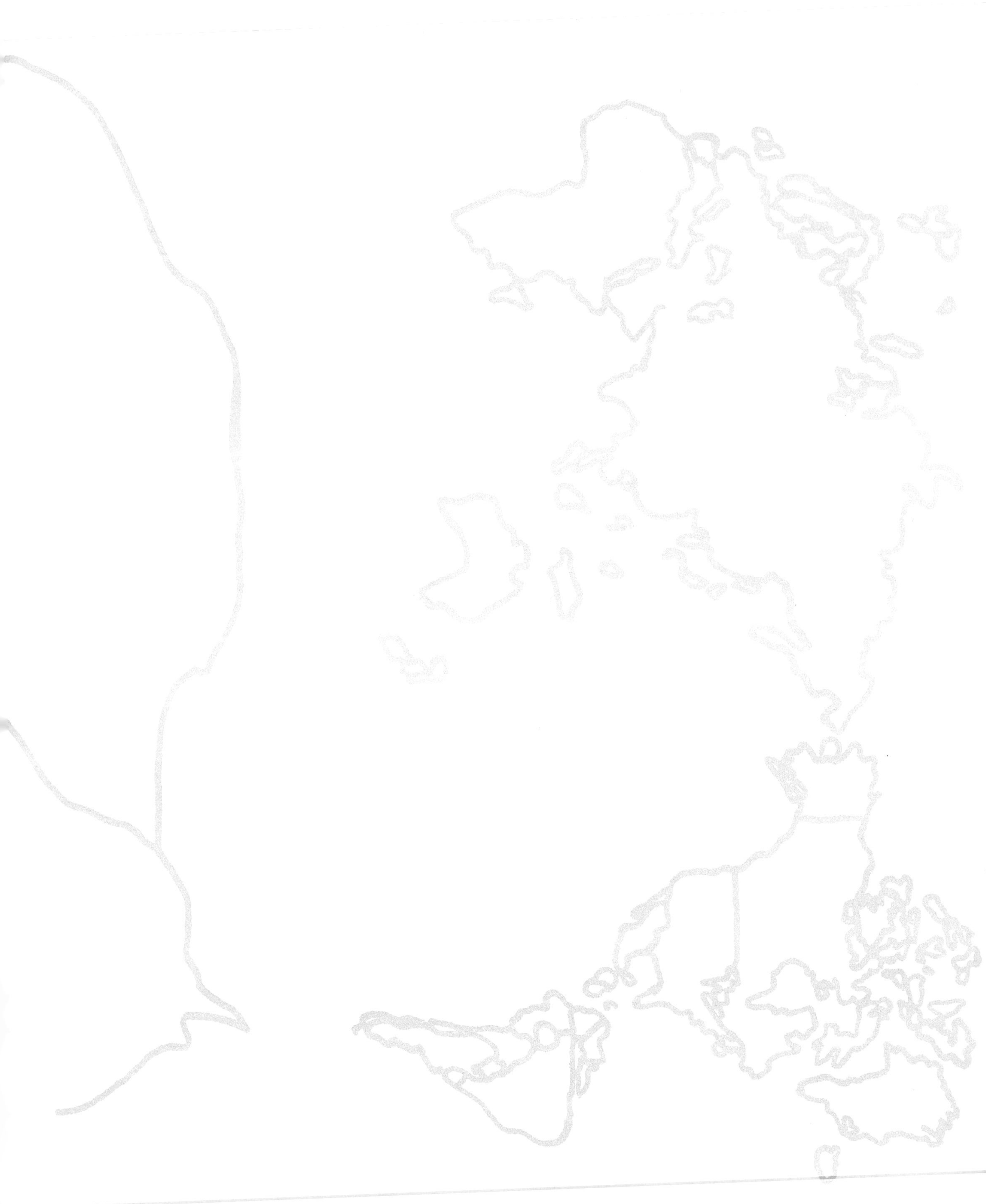

All Grown Up

PAGE FOR ENTRY BY CHILD WHEN HE/SHE GROWS UP

www.ingramcontent.com/pod-product-compliance
Lightning Source LLC
LaVergne TN
LVHW070150110826
845147LV00002B/360

9781426928727